A TURNING POINT BOOK

Sometimes there is a happening in our lives that changes the way we think about ourselves and sends us along a new path. These turning points can come when we are young—through a person we meet, an experience we have, a difficulty we overcome.

Since 1789, only a small number of people have been president of the United States. What has made these individuals unique? Was there a turning point in their young lives that caused them to change direction and set them on a path that led them to the White House?

—Judith St. George

To Jim, Sandy, Zach and Ted, with love.

—J.St.G.

Dedicated to the memory of my dad, George "Brud" Faulkner, 1928–2005.

—M.F.

Stand Tall, ABE LINCOLN

Judith St. George

illustrated by
Matt Faulkner

PUFFIN BOOKS
An Imprint of Penguin Group (USA)

Chapter 1. ABE IN THE BACKWOODS

Farming was hard for Thomas and Nancy Lincoln in Hardin County, Kentucky. The soil was rocky and the crops were poor. Their first farm on Nolin Creek failed. But a happy event took place on that farm on February 12, 1809. Nancy Lincoln gave birth to a son. As soon as he was born, Abe's red face puckered up in a loud squawl, and Nancy knew she had a strong, healthy baby boy.

Nancy Lincoln was tall and long-legged. Baby Abe was long-legged, too. And they had the same gray eyes. Nancy had a high forehead and a sharp, thin face. But there was nothing sharp about her. She was a warm, loving mother, who rocked Abe by the fire and sang hymns to him in a sweet, clear voice. Even when Abe and his sister, Sarah, were very young, she taught them the Bible stories that her mother had taught her. She dearly loved Abe and Sarah, and they knew it.

When Abe was two and Sarah four, the Lincolns moved ten miles away. Knob Creek ran through their new land. Sunlight sparkled off the rippling, clear water. Their new cabin had a hard-packed dirt floor, one window and a door that hung on leather hinges . . . just like their last cabin. Abe felt right at home.

But Knob Creek farm was full of surprises. A turnpike ran right past their door. Abe had a passing parade to watch: settlers in covered wagons, peddlers, traveling preachers, fast-talking politicians . . . and slaves in chains. The chains clanked and rattled. How awful to be chained up like that.

Abe was in for another surprise. His mother gave birth to a baby named Thomas. A little one for Nancy to sing to and cuddle. A playmate for three-year-old Abe. But little Thomas wasn't a red-faced, squawling baby like Abe had been. He was sickly, and Knob Creek had no doctor.

Thomas lived only a few days.

After that, Nancy's eyes always seemed sad. She grew thin and tired-looking. In the backwoods, death was part of life, and life went on. Everyone had chores. By the time Abe was six, he fetched water from the creek, swept out the fireplace, hoed weeds in the kitchen garden and gathered nuts.

Abe expected to do chores. What he didn't expect was a neighbor to give him a pink baby pig for his very own. The pig became more than a pet. Find Abe, and the pig wouldn't be far behind. By late summer he was big enough to ride. Oh, how the pig's prickly hairs tickled Abe's bare feet!

Fall arrived with golden leaves, red wild crabapples . . . and bad news. Thomas told Abe his pig was needed for the family's winter pork. That couldn't be. The pig was Abe's best playmate. If his parents thought slavery was cruel, killing his pig was just as cruel. Abe ran away. For two days, he hid in the woods. But nothing changed his pet's terrible fate.

The joy of summer was over. Winter set in. Cold winds crept through chinks in the log walls. Nancy drew Abe and Sarah up to the warmth of the fire logs. Taking out the family Bible, she taught them their letters. Abe had a marvel of a memory. He was so eager to learn that once he mastered a letter, he never forgot it.

Chapter 2. ABE IN SCHOOL

Wonder of wonders, an ABC school opened in Knob Creek. Though Thomas would have to pay in money, food or clothes, six-year-old Abe and eight-year-old Sarah were going. In the backwoods, most settlers couldn't read or write. Thomas could write his name. Nancy could read but couldn't write. She signed her name with an X. Abe and Sarah were going to grow up smarter than that.

Abe's big day arrived. But thinking about school wasn't the same as going to school. What if everyone else already knew how to read and write? What if the older boys teased or bullied him? It was too late to back out. Scrubbed from head to toe, Abe and Sarah joined the passing parade for the two-mile walk to school.

Knob Creek school was a one-room cabin. Abe and Sarah sat on a split log bench with the other boys and girls. Lessons began. Schoolmaster Riney paced up and down as everyone repeated the alphabet after him. Out loud. "A-B-C-D-E . . ." Arithmetic, called ciphering, was next. Out loud. "One and one equals two. Two and two equals four . . ." What a racket! No wonder this was called a blab school. But if someone wasn't blabbing, out came Schoolmaster Riney's switch.

Abe and Sarah finished the day in fine fettle. They already knew their letters. Plenty of others couldn't read or write either. And Abe wasn't teased or bullied. Abe wanted to be called Abraham. He was proud to be named for his grandfather, Abraham Lincoln. But "Abe" it was, and always would be. Some dunderheads couldn't even get that straight. They called him "Abe Linkhorn."

Austin Gollaher became Abe's very first friend. They climbed trees. Abe always tried to go the highest. They fished in Knob Creek. Abe always tried to catch the biggest. One day, Abe fell in Knob Creek. He couldn't swim! Austin lay on a log and reached out his hand. Holding on tight, Abe clambered to safety. That was the day Abe discovered what it meant to have a good friend.

In school, Abe learned to print his name and spell. Thomas bought Abe and Sarah a schoolbook to share—*Dilworth's Speller*. It was chock-full of words, grammar, poetry, geography, history, Bible stories and fables. The fables had animal pictures. They were the first pictures Abe had ever seen.

When warm south winds blew, school closed. Every hand was needed for spring planting. Abe rode the horse that pulled his father's plow. In summer he shucked the corn and weeded the garden. At least he could go barefoot and bareheaded.

Abe's father cleared trees, plowed the fields and planted crops. Thomas was known far and wide for his great strength. He wasn't very tall, but he was stocky and broad-chested. He had straight, coarse black hair and dark skin. Abe did, too.

After the fall harvests were in, school opened again. Seven-year-old Abe was bright . . . and stubborn. He liked reading best. But he wouldn't begin a new lesson until he made sure he understood the last one. That was Abe. He wrote down his

lessons on a board with a lump of coal. When the board got all black, he shaved it off and started over.

As soon as the trees began to green up, school closed again. How could Abe ever learn everything he wanted to know if he went to school "by littles"? He'd have to practice his reading at home until school opened next winter.

But next winter wasn't to be. Abe's father, Thomas, thought he owned his land free and clear. He didn't. Someone else claimed it. Well then, Thomas would buy land from the government in slave-free Indiana that would be his forever. He would move his family to Indiana and start all over, that's what he'd do.

Chapter 3. ABE IN LITTLE PIGEON CREEK

Abe went with his mother to visit Baby Thomas's grave. If Abe felt sad saying good-bye to Knob Creek, how much sadder his mother must have felt saying good-bye to Baby Thomas forever.

Little Pigeon Creek was almost a hundred miles from Knob Creek. It snowed. A brutal December wind blew. Abe rode with Sarah in an open wagon, huddled under a bearskin blanket. Would he ever be warm again?

A ferry ride across the ice-caked Ohio River and the Lincolns were in Indiana.

For sixteen miles, Abe and Sarah's wagon bucked and bounced over a frozen dirt trail. They passed only a few log cabins. Abe didn't see anyone his age. Who would be his friends? Dark forests of oak and hickory crowded in on them. To Abe, this looked like bear and wolf country. It was.

The Lincolns' land was all dark forests, too. More bears! More wolves! Thomas had earlier put up a small three-sided log and brush shelter called a half-faced camp. The fourth side was open to the wind and weather. The Lincolns moved in and kept a fire going. At night Abe heard wildcats scream and wolves howl. He closed his eyes tight and pressed close to his mother and father.

Thomas built a log cabin for his family. One winter day a flock of turkeys strutted by. Abe grabbed his father's rifle, stuck it through a crack and shot a turkey. His mother was delighted. Turkey for the stew pot. Abe wasn't delighted. Shooting that turkey was as cruel as killing his pet pig. Abe promised himself he would never again kill another large creature, and he never did.

School? Little Pigeon Creek had none. Friends? Abe had no time to find any. Still, Abe heard his mother singing as she built up the morning fire. He smelled corn cakes frying and sassafras tea brewing. His mother could make even Little Pigeon Creek into a home.

At last Abe found a friend, Henry Brooner. Abe rode with Henry to the gristmill to have corn ground into meal. Abe did most of the talking. He was quite a storyteller. Henry was always all ears to hear Abe's tales.

One day, Abe hitched up his old mare to the arm of the gristmill. She was pokey and Abe switched her. Crack! She kicked Abe in the forehead. Down he went. Was he dead? No, he was still breathing. Abe was as tough as hickory. He was soon back riding with Henry, and still talking a mile a minute.

To everyone's delight, that fall his mother's Aunt Elizabeth and Uncle Thomas Sparrow and their nephew, Dennis Hanks, moved to Little Pigeon Creek. Abe was happy to see eighteen-year-old Dennis. Back in Kentucky, Dennis could always tickle Abe's funny bone with a good yarn.

But the joking ended when milk sickness struck. No one knew that when cows ate the white snakeroot plant, their milk was poisoned. Thomas and Elizabeth Sparrow fell sick. So did Henry Brooner's mother. Nancy nursed all three, but all three died. Dennis Hanks moved in with the Lincolns. It was a sad time. Then Nancy took sick. Milk sickness! Abe felt helpless . . . and terrified. His mother wouldn't die. She couldn't! But she was dying and she knew it. "Be good and kind to your father—to one another and to the world," Nancy told Abe and Sarah. "I want you to live as I have taught you."

Nancy Lincoln died on October 5, 1818. Thomas sawed the planks for her coffin, while nine-year-old Abe whittled the coffin pegs. It was the hardest thing he ever had to do. Nancy Lincoln was buried not far from the Lincolns' cabin.

Abe couldn't believe his mother was gone. He would never again see her loving smile. He would never again snuggle up to her by the fire to practice his reading. He would never, ever forget his "angel mother."

Chapter 4. ABE IN PINCHING TIMES

How could Abe get along without his mother? She'd always been the quiet, loving center of the family. Now Thomas, Abe, Sarah and Dennis were on their own. Sarah tried to take over her mother's chores. But Sarah had never cooked and didn't know how. Overwhelmed and sad, she spent most of her time weeping by the fire.

Abe didn't sit by the fire and weep, but his world had turned dark, too. How could he sound out new words without her listening ear? Heartsick as Abe felt, he and Dennis tried to cheer up Sarah. They brought her a turtle and a baby raccoon. But nothing helped.

Nothing helped Abe either. His mother had given him affection, tenderness and warmth. All that was gone. Thomas had never fussed over Abe and Sarah, and he didn't fuss now. Abe and Sarah's greatest comfort was reading the Bible out loud as their mother had taught them to do.

Nancy's death had been such a cruel blow that now Abe couldn't bear any kind of cruelty. He shouted at boys who heaped hot coals on turtles to force them out of their shells. He chased off youngsters who tortured cats.

At least he didn't have to watch slaves in chains clank by. Indiana didn't allow slavery.

Thomas went about his farm chores in silence. Abe didn't talk much either. What was there to say? And just look at how they were living. Even Abe could see the cabin's dirt floor never got swept . . . nothing was picked up . . . the skillet and stew pot were burned . . . his clothes were torn and filthy. When did he last comb his hair? He didn't know or care.

Hardest for Abe was to wake up to a cold and silent cabin. Ashes filled the fireplace. There was no soft voice singing or warm morning smells of corn cakes and sassafras tea. Breakfast was leftover scraps. Abe was almost always hungry.

Winter passed into spring, spring into summer, and then it was fall again. What a gloomy year! Abe recalled that time as the "bitterest agony." Thomas finally realized they couldn't go on this way. He was lonely. His ragamuffin children were living like little animals. He told Abe, Sarah and Dennis that he was going back to Kentucky to find a wife. One cold November day he bid them farewell.

A wife? But if their father brought back a wife, she would be Abe and Sarah's stepmother. No one could take the place of their "angel mother." No one!

Weeks passed. Thomas didn't return. Dennis hunted to keep food on the table. He and Abe fed the livestock, milked the cow and kept the fire going. Bathe? Wash clothes? Clean the cabin? Prepare a decent meal? None of those things happened.

Abe and Dennis tried to keep Sarah's spirits up, but their spirits were as low as hers. Soon after dusk darkened the skies, they went to bed. What else was there to do? Read, maybe, but Abe's grease lamp shed little light.

Winter arrived with icy rain and snow. The roof leaked. The wind whistled through the cracks. They were hungry. Abe had never known such "pinching times."

Still, there was no sign of Thomas.

Chapter 5. ABE UP IN THE AIR

One December day, Abe and Sarah heard a commotion of horses and voices outside. Their father was home. He'd come back with a farm wagon piled high with furniture. And a wife. Three children were perched on the wagon with her.

Sally Lincoln was tall and big-boned with a wide smile. She beamed and waved to Abe and Sarah. She didn't seem to notice that Abe's long limbs stuck out of his greasy butternut jeans and filthy tow shirt. Or that Sarah's dress was in tatters. She opened her heart and arms to the two sad-looking children. Sarah flew into them. Not Abe. He always took his time making up his mind about anything new, and what was newer than a new stepmother?

Back in Kentucky, Thomas had known Sally for years. She was widowed, too. Now Sally introduced her children to Abe and Sarah. There was Elizabeth, she was twelve, Matilda was eight and John D. five. Abe was tall for ten. He towered over little John D. They were one family now.

Nineteen-year-old Dennis and Thomas unloaded the wagon. A dresser, beds, mattresses, clothes chest, spinning wheel, table, chairs, pots, even knives, forks and spoons piled up. Abe had never seen such fancy furniture.

First things first. Sally filled the horse trough with water. Abe and Sarah knew what that meant. A bath. But baths were for summertime, not December. There was no arguing with Sally. Abe and Sarah shivered through a good, hard scrub.

Cleaning the dirty cabin came next. Happy not to be in charge, Sarah pitched in. Abe carried water back and forth from the creek, but he didn't join in the chatter. He needed time to get used to Sally. Not only was she big and broad-shouldered, but she also had a loud, booming voice. Abe's mother had been tall and slender, and her voice had been soft. How could a stepmother with three ready-made children have any love left over for them? And how could eight people and all that furniture fit into their one-room cabin?

Sally had her own ideas. She had Thomas build a loft with a ladder of pegs for Abe, John D. and Dennis. Sally kept Thomas and Dennis hustling. Build a bed for the three girls . . . lay down a wood floor . . . fix the leaky roof . . . cut out a window . . . hang a door . . . whitewash the walls.

Right off, Sally announced she couldn't read or write. So Abe was struck dumb when she unpacked a pile of books. And what books! *Aesop's Fables, Pilgrim's Progress, Arabian Nights, Life of George Washington, Robinson Crusoe.* Sally must have seen Abe's eyes light up. She told him he was welcome to read any book he wanted.

But chores didn't wait for books. Winter was for clearing land, felling trees and taking out stumps. All the time Abe chopped and burned, the image of Sally's magical books lingered. If only he could use his head instead of his hands.

And then almost-eleven-year-old Abe did start using his head. Most Little

Pigeon Creek settlers couldn't read or write. They began to stop by the Lincolns' cabin to have Abe read their mail and write their letters. Abe learned a lot. He learned that under their easy smiles, most people were worried, ill, in debt, homesick or troubled. It was a lesson he never forgot.

Sally understood Abe from the start. Some people thought Abe was slow. Far from it. Yes, he took his own sweet time figuring things out. That's because he wanted everything straight in his head before he made a decision or spoke out. Sally loved Abe and was sure that someday he would come to love her.

Chapter 6. ABE AND SALLY IN THE "SAME CHANNEL"

Eight mouths to feed meant more plowing, more planting, more harvesting. Abe would do everything his father told him to do, but he didn't have to like it. He often carried a book under his shirt. If his father wasn't around, he stopped at the end of a plow furrow. The horse rested . . . and Abe read.

Sally knew how much eleven-year-old Abe itched to read and study. She tried not to play favorites, but if she had a favorite, it was Abe. Of course she wasn't smart like Abe. But in some ways they were alike. "His mind and mine, what little I had, seemed to run together, move in the same channel," Sally said.

Would he like to read to her after supper as she mended and patched? He would. Abe spent many an evening reading to Sally . . . and anyone else who joined them by the fire.

Sinbad the Sailor legends were the best. In one story, Sinbad was on a desert island where a giant bird lived. When the bird flew, its wings blotted out the sun and the earth turned "dull and dark." Abe knew all about "dull and dark," though his world hadn't been so "dull and dark" of late.

Abe's world grew even brighter. A blab school was opening in Little Pigeon Creek. Sally got Thomas to allow all five children to go. None of her babes was going to end up an ignoramus like her. Abe could hardly believe his good luck. He was going to school again after almost four years.

Abe and school were a perfect fit. David Turnham became his friend. So did
Nathaniel Grigsby. (Abe was the tallest.) They played prisoner's base and hare-
and-hounds. They ran footraces. (Abe was the fastest.) If Schoolmaster Crawford
wasn't watching, they wrestled. (Abe was the strongest.)

Some of the boys fought and quarreled. Not Abe. He settled quarrels. And
he was tops at reading, writing and ciphering, plus he won every spelling bee.
He could also be a cutup. When his friends stole a melon from Thomas's melon
patch, Abe shared in the feast. He penned in his copybook: "Abraham Lincoln his
hand and pen he will be good but god knows When."

On winter nights, Abe lay by the fire and studied. But his father found chores for him to do. Shell those hickory nuts . . . whittle new pegs for the loft ladder . . . sharpen your ax.

It was too much for Sally. From now on, Thomas wasn't to pester Abe when he was studying, especially with chores that could wait until the morrow. School was about to shut down for spring planting, and Abe needed all the book-learning he could get.

If Thomas was surprised, Abe was even more surprised. Good-natured Sally laid down the law like that for him? Wait a minute—she had stood up for him before. She'd given him all her books, hadn't she? She had listened to him read night after night. And good luck hadn't gotten him back into school. Sally had. She had even meshed two families into one. Why, right from the start, it was Sally's love and caring that had swept away his "dull and dark" world.

It wasn't that Abe forgot his own mother. He didn't. But Sally's belief in Abe's future promise to overcome his "pinching times" and schooling "by littles" gave him the space to grow and learn beyond his hardscrabble backwoods beginnings. He gained confidence to take his sense of fairness, his careful way of thinking, his hatred of cruelty and his ability to settle quarrels out into the world.

As a boy, Abe had climbed from peg to peg up to his loft bed. As a man, Abraham Lincoln climbed up out of poverty the same way, peg by peg—from riverman to store clerk to postmaster to surveyor to lawyer. But not even Abraham Lincoln himself could have guessed how far his promise would take him . . . or what it would mean to both him and his country.

Abraham Lincoln was born to Thomas and Nancy Lincoln in a backwoods one-room log cabin on February 12, 1809, in Hardin County, Kentucky. Soon after, the family moved to the wilderness of Indiana. All in all, Lincoln had one year of schooling.

Lincoln's first job was on a Mississippi River flatboat, followed by work as a handyman, militia volunteer in the Black Hawk War, store clerk, postmaster and county surveyor, all the while studying law. In 1834 he was elected to the Illinois Assembly, serving for eight years. After he became a lawyer in 1836, he opened an office in Springfield, Illinois. Elected to the U.S. House of Representatives in 1846, he served one term.

Over the next ten years, Lincoln became prominent in Republican Illinois politics. In 1858 he debated Stephen Douglas for election to the U. S. Senate seat from Illinois. Although he lost, the debates earned Lincoln national fame, and in 1860 he was elected the sixteenth president of the United States.

For the next four years, Lincoln presided over the Civil War fought between the Union (North) and the Confederacy (South), which resulted in some 600,000 American deaths. In 1863 Lincoln issued his Emancipation Proclamation, freeing slaves in Confederate territory. Ten months later, Lincoln gave his timeless Gettysburg Address at the dedication of a national cemetery.

The "Great Emancipator" won a second term in 1864. His plans to reconcile the North and South with generous peace terms never happened. On April 14, 1865, only days after the Confederacy surrendered, Abraham Lincoln was shot at Ford's Theatre in Washington by John Wilkes Booth. He died the next day.

BIBLIOGRAPHY

Bial, Raymond. *Where Lincoln Walked.* New York: Walker And Co., 1997.

Davenport, Don. *In Lincoln's Footsteps.* Madison, Wisconsin: Prairie Oak Press, 1991.

Fleming, Thomas J. *The Living Land of Lincoln.* New York: Reader's Digest Press, 1980.

Judson, Clara Ingram. *Abraham Lincoln: Friend of the People.* Chicago: Wilcox and Follett Co., 1950.

Lorant, Stefan. *The Life of Abraham Lincoln: A Short Illustrated Biography.* New York: McGraw-Hill Co., Inc., 1954.

North, Sterling. *Abe Lincoln: Log Cabin to White House.* New York: Random House, 1956.

Oates, Stephen B. *With Malice Toward None: The Life of Abraham Lincoln.* New York: Harper & Row, 1977.

Thomas, Benjamin P. *Abraham Lincoln: A Biography.* New York: Alfred A. Knopf, 1952.

United States Department of the Interior, National Park Service. *Lincoln Boyhood.* Lincoln, Nebraska: Lincoln Boyhood National Memorial pamphlet.

Warren, Louis A. *Lincoln's Parentage & Childhood.* New York: The Century Co., 1926.

———. *Lincoln's Youth: Indiana Years, Seven to Twenty-one, 1816–1830.* New York: Appleton, Century, Crofts, Inc., 1959.

Wilson, Douglas L., and Rodney O. Davis, eds. *Herndon's Informants: Letters, Interviews, and Statements about Abraham Lincoln.* Urbana: University of Illinois Press, 1998.

Patricia Lee Gauch, Editor

PUFFIN BOOKS
Published by the Penguin Group
Penguin Group (USA) LLC
375 Hudson Street
New York, New York 10014

USA * Canada * UK * Ireland * Australia
New Zealand * India * South Africa * China

penguin.com
A Penguin Random House Company

First published in the United States of America by Philomel Books,
a division of Penguin Young Readers Group, 2008
Published by Puffin Books, an imprint of Penguin Young Readers Group, 2014

Text copyright © 2008 by Judith St. George
Illustrations copyright © 2008 by Matt Faulkner

THE LIBRARY OF CONGRESS HAS CATALOGED THE PHILOMEL BOOKS EDITION AS FOLLOWS:
St. George, Judith, date.
Stand tall, Abe Lincoln / Judith St. George ; illustrated by Matt Faulkner.
p. cm.
ISBN 978-0-399-24174-1 (hardcover)
Includes bibliographical references. 1. Lincoln, Abraham, 1809–1865—Juvenile literature.
2. Presidents—United States—Biography—Juvenile literature.
I. Faulkner, Matt, ill. II. Title.
E457.905.S68 2008
973.7092—dc22 [B]
2006024877

Puffin Books ISBN 978-0-14-751447-9

Manufactured in China

3 5 7 9 10 8 6 4 2